Bibi
and
Rumi

Written by Shagufta K Iqbal

Illustrated by Koustubha Jagadeesh

Collins

Bibi is no ordinary girl.
And Rumi is no ordinary cat.
So, their paths were destined to cross,
when Bibi and Mum moved to a new flat.

It was an immense change,
moving to a new neighbourhood.
Some days Bibi felt bad;
some days Bibi felt good.
And when she was with her dad,
she missed her mum.
When she was with her mum,
she missed her dad.
Nothing about her new life was much fun.

3

One moment Bibi felt excited;
the next moment she felt nervous.
Her stomach swirled,
like a washing machine,
with soapy bubbles of:

I can't wait to decorate my room green
and
I don't like it here!
I miss my old home too!

Her emotions were overwhelming,
they just grew and grew,
until she didn't know how to feel,
or what to do.

She wandered the playground feeling lonely,
She was quiet and felt shy in her new school –
nothing here felt homely.

She struggled to speak to anyone new,
and missed her old friends.
No one understood what she was going through.

The loneliness clung to Bibi,
she was as invisible as a ghost,
as if she did not exist,
or lived in a parallel universe –
hidden behind a cloud of mist.
She wanted to cry and shout.

Then one day,
bored,
playing by herself,
a little lost and forlorn,
Bibi sat in the garden,
where it was bright and warm.

Suddenly, at the garden's edge
she saw a small dark shadow,
hiding in the green hedge.

Feeling bold and brave,
she edged closer,
and mustered a nervous wave.

Out of the blossoming bushes,
the dark shadow slowly sat,
revealing itself as …
a brilliant midnight blue cat!
At first, he slowly sniffed and crept,
made his way across the lawn.

Suddenly, he jumped and leapt!
Then stretched with a lazy yawn.
The cat came and sat by Bibi,
looking peaceful and carefree.
As comforting as warm buttered toast,
Bibi cuddled this welcome new friend
and no longer felt like a ghost.

Bibi named him Rumi.
Now her days weren't
sad and gloomy.
Finally, Bibi had something to look forward to!

They played "Astronauts"
and explored far away galaxies.
She taught Rumi new tricks,
her amazing sidekick.
Bibi and Rumi forever!

Happiness can be a simple thing,
a smile from a friend, a warm hug.
like the sun shining down on you,
a bright, brilliant beam,
making you feel loved and seen.

Then suddenly, one day, Rumi didn't come ...
Nor the next day,
or the day after that.
Had Rumi found somewhere else to play?
Or – had he been cat-napped?

Bibi tried to find out.
She made "Lost Cat" posters.
She looked under cars; up in the trees.
She was beginning to feel helpless.
She wondered why happiness
came and left in such great waves.

Bibi felt abandoned
and friendless once again,
like a floating astronaut
lost and forgotten in outer space.

Bibi, with posters in hand,
was determined to find Rumi.
Everything was planned.
She stuck posters on lampposts,
corner-shop doors and bulletin boards.
Surely, word would get around,
and Rumi would be found.

As Bibi got to work,
she couldn't help but notice,
stuck on lampposts, doors and boards
were other "Lost Cat" posters.
An image of a cheeky cat,
strikingly similar to Rumi.
Round and fat,
the exact same size!
Fur the same midnight blue,
with emerald green eyes.

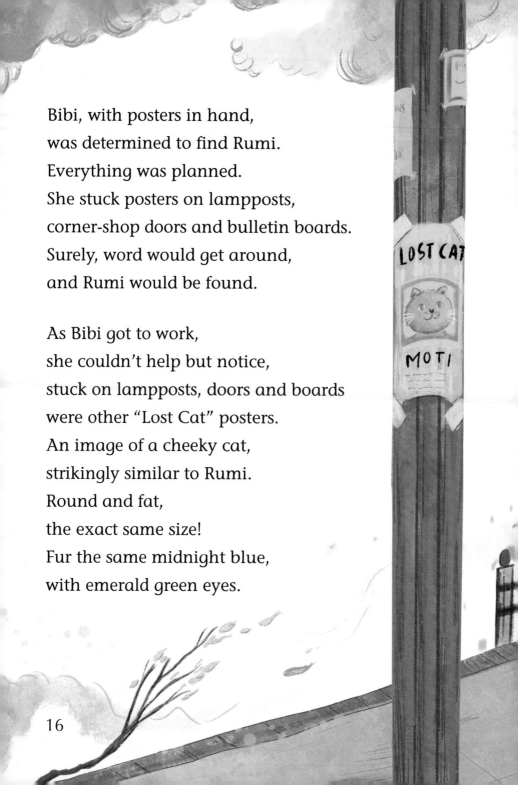

The other poster read:

Moti, our much-loved cat, is missing.
If you see him, please call Rajveer Singh.

The posters were plastered everywhere!
All looking for Rumi,
but Rumi had disappeared.
How confusing it must be
for one little cat
to have two homes.

Bibi thought:

He must feel just like I do.
Sometimes I live with Mum.
Sometimes I live with Dad.
Sometimes I feel like hiding, too!

They walked to Rajveer's house.
and knocked politely on the door.
They stood and patiently waited,
feeling a little unsure.
Finally, the door opened.
And in a pair of dungarees,
stood a boy,
who Bibi recognised
with a little unease.

The boy smiled, bright and warm,
"Hey! I know you!" he exclaimed.

Rajveer told them about Moti,
his grandma's beloved cat.
How much joy Moti brings her and
how sad she had been
since Moti had gone away,
nowhere to be seen.

Bibi promised to help,
to meet and make a plan.
They would find Moti,
and return him safe and sound.

Bibi felt full of energy,
excited to be part of a team.
No longer lonely or nervous.
Now she had a purpose.

There were many days of searching,
but without any luck.
Where could Moti be lurking?

One long week dragged by.
It seemed they were searching in vain.
Searching with no hope.
But then, one day …
while waiting for a train,
Bibi spotted something –
a movement, a flicker …
In a disused old ticket booth
hidden away
a familiar cat crept between the shadows.

"*It's Rumi!*" shouted Bibi.

A train station can be a dangerous place.
You must take care when walking,
and don't shoot off on a wild cat chase!
So Mum and Bibi asked for help.

A staff member, keys in hand,
unlocked the ticket booth,
and walked into the dark room.
The door shut behind him.
Bibi felt like she was waiting forever,
her breath was caught in her chest.

Finally, he returned to the platform.
and Bibi felt so relieved and blessed.
The staff member held in his arms,
a shabby-looking cardboard box.
In it, wrapped up warm,
a rather dirty-looking Rumi,
all weathered and worn.

"*You found him!*" cheered Bibi.

"*Him?*" The staff member looked puzzled.

Because to Bibi's great surprise,
Rumi lay with a litter of kittens,
all staring with emerald green eyes!

Rumi, also known as Moti,
was returned to Grandma Singh.
Rajveer and Bibi gained a kitten each,
which was the most wonderful thing!
They named them Mr Waffles and Little Rumi.
Grandma Singh thanked them for their support.

The rest of that summer holiday,
Bibi, Rajveer, Moti, Mr Waffles, and little Rumi,
would meet up to play!
Bibi learnt it takes time
to make friends in new places.
But when you do, it really is worth it.
Bibi was excited about the future!

She learnt that change can be tough,
that distance can make you lonely.
But friendship and family is enough.
It doesn't matter where you live,
or how unpredictable life can be,
what matters is how much love you can give.
Through Moti, Bibi realised
that *new* doesn't have to mean *scary*,
new can mean more people to love,
more friendships to be made,
if only you can be brave enough
to look beyond feeling sad.

Making friends

happy

lonely

abandoned

brave

unsure

relieved

Ideas for reading

Written by Jonny Walker
Specialist Teacher and Educational Consultant

Reading objectives
- learn that poetry can be used to tell a story
- understand how poets can use rhyme and near-rhyme
- understand how poets can use simile

Spoken language objectives
- ask relevant questions to extend their understanding and knowledge
- use relevant strategies to build their vocabulary
- articulate and justify answers, arguments and opinions
- give well-structured descriptions, explanations and narratives for different purposes, including for expressing feelings
- participate in performances

Curriculum links: Relationships education: Caring friendships; Families and people who care for me

Interest words: change, sidekick, friendships, rhymes, near-rhymes, simile

Word count: 1133

Talk before reading
- Look at the cover together and read the title and blurb. Establish that Bibi is the girl and Rumi is the cat from the image on the cover. Discuss the setting on the cover and that the garden appears to be in a city.
- Point out that we know from the blurb that Bibi and her mum have just moved into a new flat. Discuss what changes this might mean for Bibi. Consider together how it feels when something changes, giving examples where possible.

Support personal responses
- Take time to discuss the poem after you have read it. Use the following questions or ask your own.
  - o Is the way we care about pets the same as the way we care about people?
  - o Can you think of a time you have felt a bit like Rumi did at the start of the story?